Blastoff! Readers are carefully developed by literacy experts to build reading stamina and move students toward fluency by combining standards-based content with developmentally appropriate text.

Level 1 provides the most support through repetition of high-frequency words, light text, predictable sentence patterns, and strong visual support.

Level 2 offers early readers a bit more challenge through varied sentences, increased text load, and text-supportive special features.

Level 3 advances early-fluent readers toward fluency through increased text load, less reliance on photos, advancing concepts, longer sentences, and more complex special features.

★ **Blastoff! Universe**

Reading Level — Grade K → Grades 1–3 → Grade 4

This edition first published in 2024 by Bellwether Media, Inc.

No part of this publication may be reproduced in whole or in part without written permission of the publisher. For information regarding permission, write to Bellwether Media, Inc., Attention: Permissions Department, 6012 Blue Circle Drive, Minnetonka, MN 55343.

Library of Congress Cataloging-in-Publication Data

Names: Davies, Monika, author.
Title: Denmark / by Monika Davies.
Description: Minneapolis, MN : Bellwether Media, Inc., 2024. | Series: Blastoff! Readers: Countries of the World | Includes bibliographical references and index. | Audience: Ages 5-7 | Audience: Grades 2-3 | Summary: "Relevant images match informative text in this introduction to Denmark. Intended for students in kindergarten through third grade"– Provided by publisher.
Identifiers: LCCN 2023046580 (print) | LCCN 2023046581 (ebook) | ISBN 9798886877939 (library binding) | ISBN 9798886878875 (ebook)
Subjects: LCSH: Denmark–Juvenile literature.
Classification: LCC DL109 .D38 2024 (print) | LCC DL109 (ebook) | DDC 948.9–dc23/eng/20231012
LC record available at https://lccn.loc.gov/2023046580
LC ebook record available at https://lccn.loc.gov/2023046581

Text copyright © 2024 by Bellwether Media, Inc. BLASTOFF! READERS and associated logos are trademarks and/or registered trademarks of Bellwether Media, Inc.

Editor: Rachael Barnes   Series Design: Gabriel Hilger   Book Designer: Kathleen Petelinsek
Printed in the United States of America, North Mankato, MN.

Table of Contents

All About Denmark	4
Land and Animals	6
Life in Denmark	12
Denmark Facts	20
Glossary	22
To Learn More	23
Index	24

All About Denmark

Copenhagen

Denmark is in northern Europe. It is part of **Scandinavia**. Copenhagen is the capital.

Denmark is known as one of the world's happiest countries!

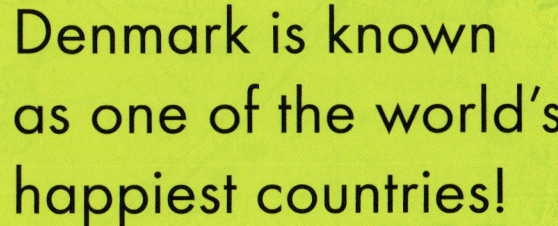

Land and Animals

Most of Denmark is a **peninsula**. Lowlands cover this land. Cliffs and beaches line the western coast.

Denmark has about 1,400 islands. Most have low hills. Seas border the country.

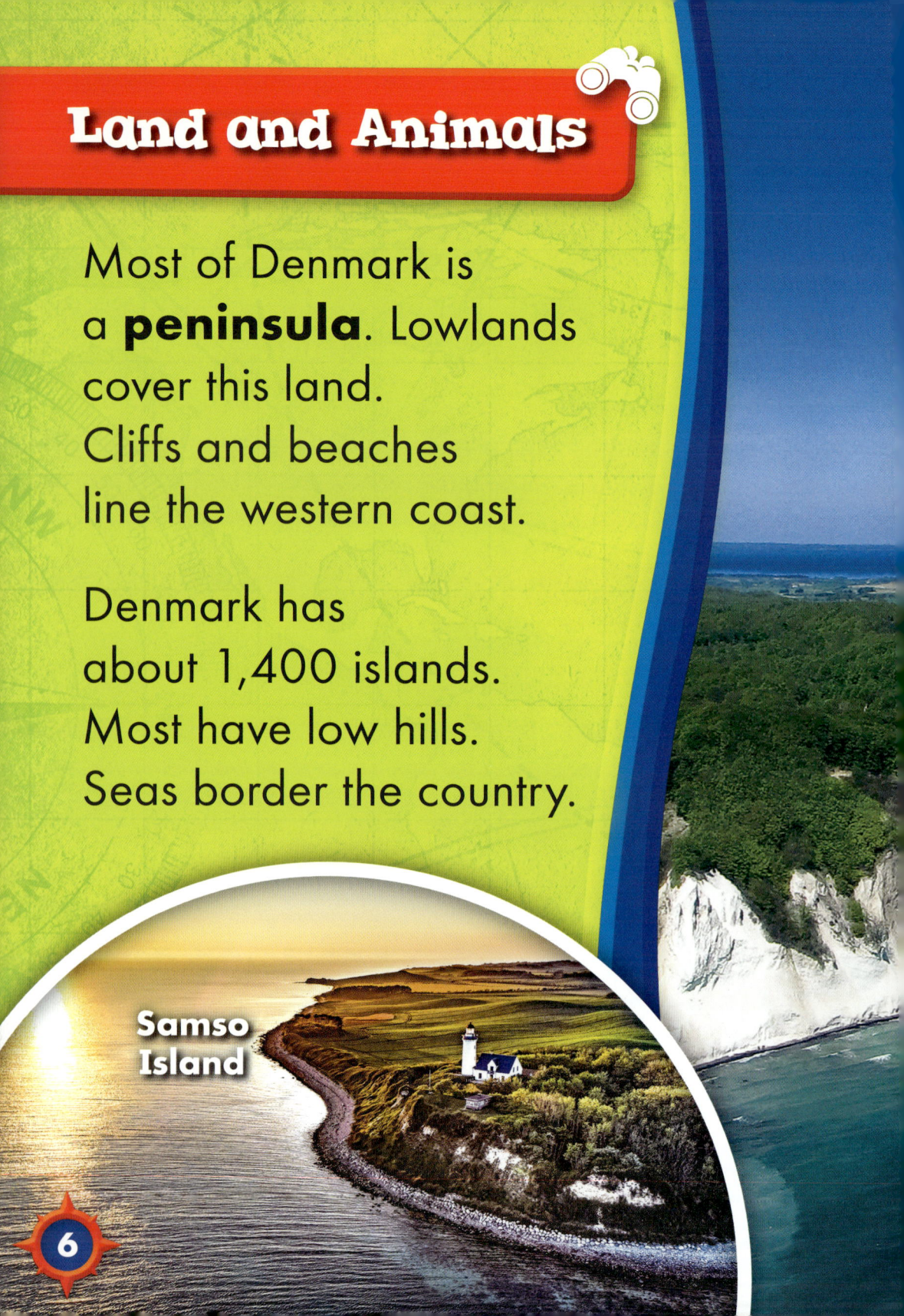

Samso Island

Mons Klint

Size: around 3.7 miles (6 kilometers) long
Famous For: a long white chalk cliff by the Baltic Sea

summer

The seas keep Denmark's **climate** mild. Rain falls all year.

Winters can be windy and cold. Summers are warmer.

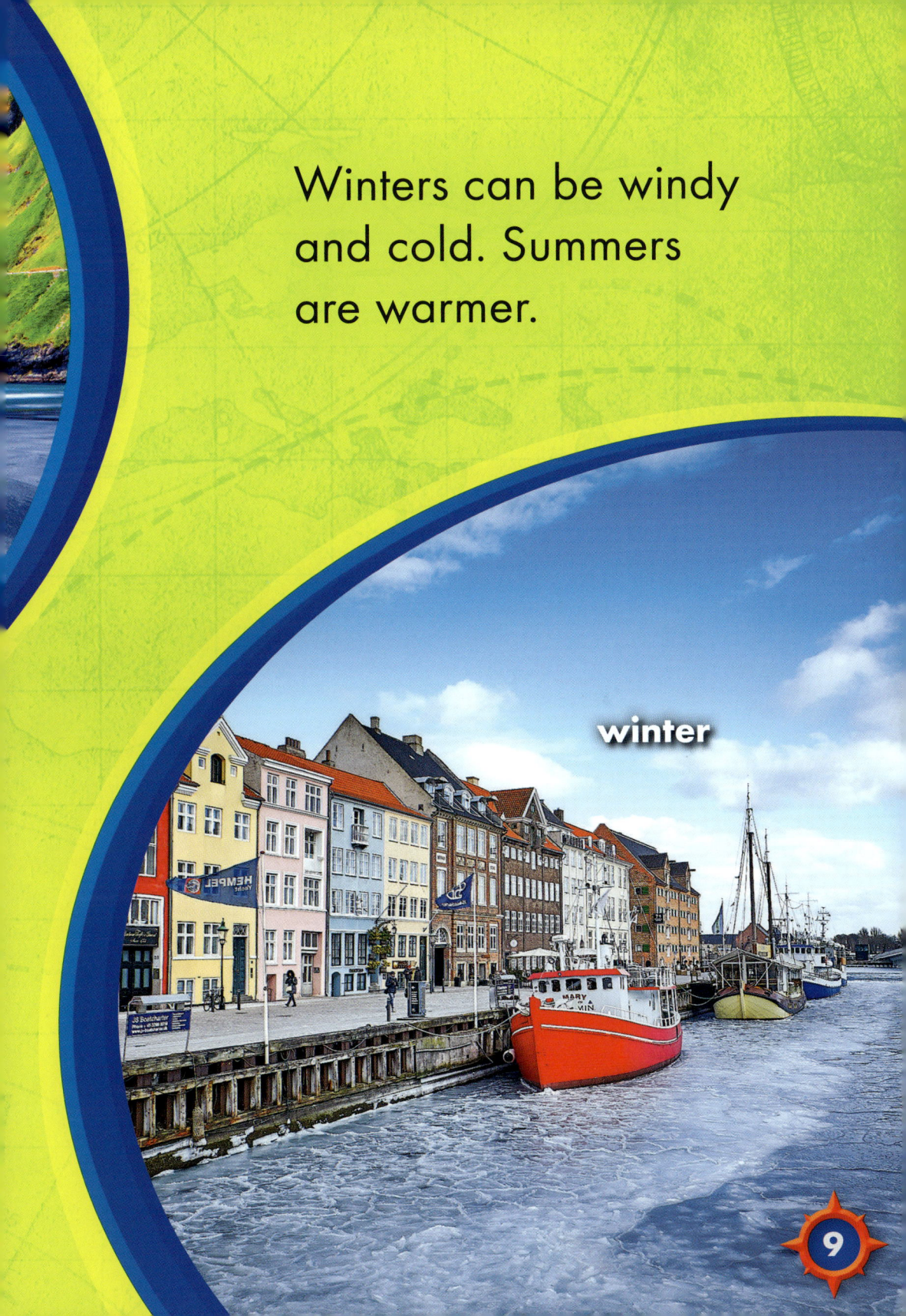

winter

Many animals call Denmark home. Roe deer **graze** in the countryside. Hedgehogs live near towns.

western European hedgehog

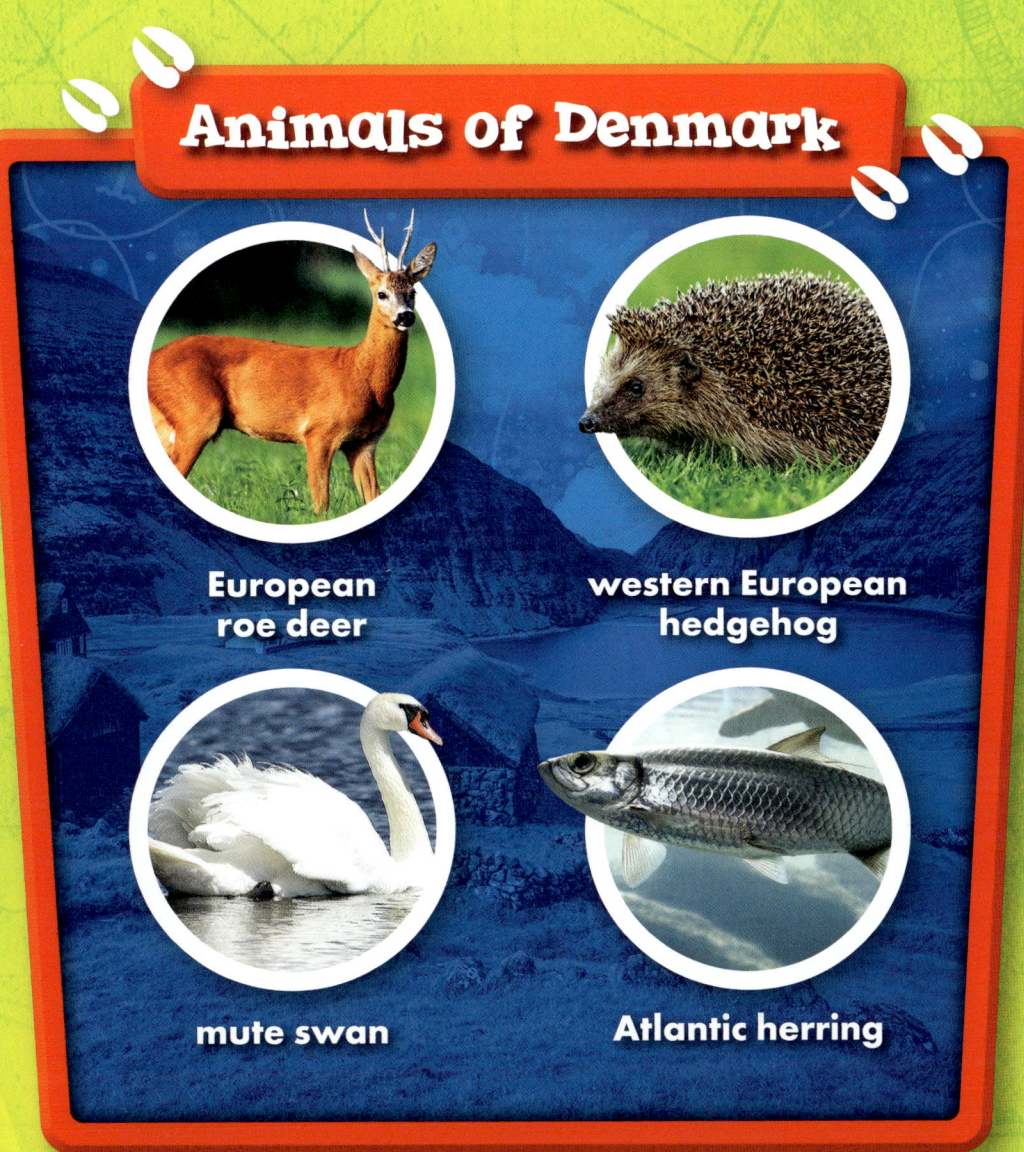

Mute swans float on lakes. Herring swim in the seas.

Life in Denmark

The people of Denmark are called Danes. Many are **Lutherans**. Nearly all Danes speak Danish and English.

Most Danes live in cities or towns. The largest city is Copenhagen.

Lutheran church

biking

Danes like to stay active. Many Danes ride bikes to work and school!

Handball and swimming are popular sports. People also enjoy kayaking.

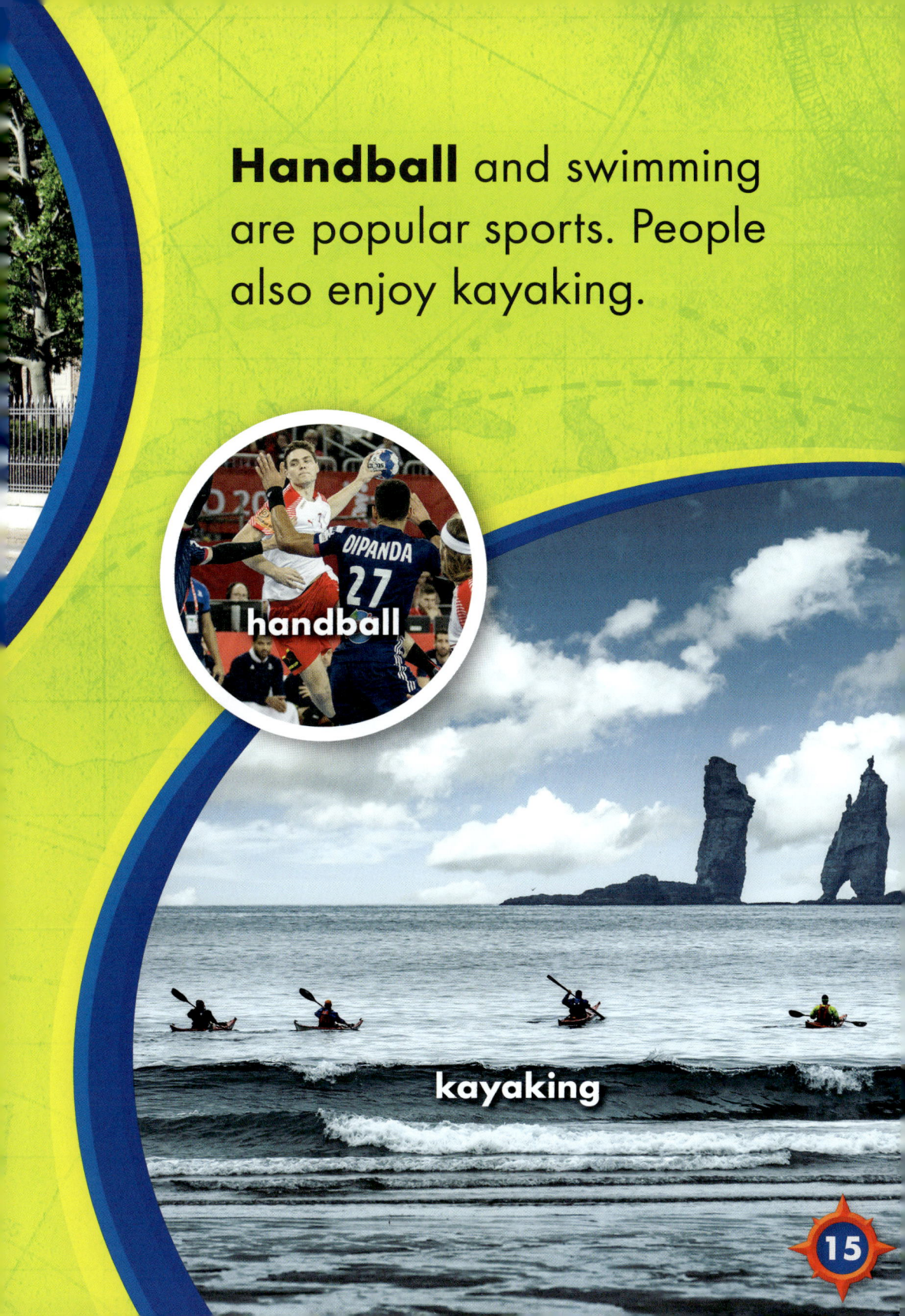

handball

kayaking

Danes eat hot dogs as a quick snack. *Smorrebrod* are open-faced sandwiches on rye bread.

Danish Foods

hot dogs

smorrebrod

stegt flaesk

kanelsnegle

hot dog stand

Stegt flaesk is a pork and potatoes dish. *Kanelsnegle* are cinnamon rolls!

Danes **celebrate** *Sankt Hans Aften* in June. Communities gather around bonfires.

Christmas is when families sing carols and dance around a tree. This winter holiday is full of warmth!

Sankt Hans Aften

Christmas

Denmark Facts

Size:
16,639 square miles
(43,095 square kilometers)

Population:
5,946,984 (2023)

National Holiday:
Constitution Day (June 5)

Main Languages:
Danish, English, Faroese, Greenlandic, German

Capital City:
Copenhagen

Famous Face

Name: Caroline Wozniacki

Famous For: top women's tennis player and winner of 30 singles titles

Religions

- Lutheran 75%
- Muslim 5%
- other 20%

Top Landmarks

Christiansborg Palace

LEGOLAND Billund

Tivoli Gardens

Glossary

celebrate—to do something special or fun for an event, occasion, or holiday

climate—the usual weather conditions of a place

graze—to eat grass or other plants growing in a field

handball—a sport where two to four players use their hands to bounce a ball against a wall

Lutherans—people who believe in a type of Christianity that follows Martin Luther and his teachings; Christianity is a religion that follows the words of Jesus Christ.

peninsula—a section of land that extends out from a larger piece of land and is almost completely surrounded by water

Scandinavia—a region of northern Europe that includes Norway, Sweden, and Denmark

To Learn More

AT THE LIBRARY

Anderson, Shannon. *Sweden*. Minneapolis, Minn.: Bellwether Media, 2024.

Brandle, Marie. *Hedgehogs*. Minneapolis, Minn.: Jump!, 2024.

Idzikowski, Lisa. *Denmark*. New York, N.Y.: Cavendish Square Publishing, 2022.

ON THE WEB

Factsurfer.com gives you a safe, fun way to find more information.

1. Go to www.factsurfer.com.

2. Enter "Denmark" into the search box and click 🔍.

3. Select your book cover to see a list of related content.

Index

animals, 10, 11
beaches, 6
biking, 14
capital
   (see Copenhagen)
Christmas, 18, 19
cities, 12
cliffs, 6, 7
climate, 8
coast, 6
Copenhagen, 4, 5, 12
countryside, 10
Danish, 12, 13
Denmark facts, 20–21
English, 12
Europe, 4
food, 16, 17
handball, 15
islands, 6
kayaking, 15

lakes, 11
lowlands, 6
Lutherans, 12
map, 5
Mons Klint, 7
peninsula, 6
people, 12, 14, 15, 16, 18
rain, 8
Sankt Hans Aften, 18
say hello, 13
Scandinavia, 4
seas, 6, 8, 11
summers, 8, 9
swimming, 15
towns, 10, 12
winters, 9, 18

The images in this book are reproduced through the courtesy of: coldsnowstorm, front cover; Nick Fox, pp. 2-3; railway fx, p. 3 (flag); Iryna Kalamurza, pp. 4-5; Rasmus Kleis, p. 6; Bob Collowan/ Wiki Commons, pp. 6-7; Andrew Mayovskyy, pp. 8-9; Double Bind Photography, p. 9; ian west/ Alamy, pp. 10-11; WildMedia, p. 11 (European roe deer); Anne Coatesy, p. 11 (western European hedgehog); Abinieks, p. 11 (mute swan); Four Oaks, p. 11 (Atlantic herring); Perekotypole, p. 12; FamVeld, pp. 12-13; Andrei Antipov, pp. 14-15; DarioZg, p. 15 (handball); Smit, p. 15 (kayaking); AS Foodstudio, p. 16 (hot dogs); OlgaBombologna, p. 16 (*smorrebrod*); starets, p. 16 (*stegt flaesk*); Angelika Heine, p. 16 (*kanelsnegle*); Frank Bach, p. 17; dba87, p. 18; imageBROKER.com GmbH & Co. KG/ Alamy, pp. 18-19; titoOnz, p. 20 (flag); Jimmie48 PHotography, p. 20 (Caroline Wozniacki); eskystudio, p. 21 (Christiansborg Palace); Anna Soelberg, p. 21 (LEGOLAND Billund); Andrij Vatsyk, p. 21 (Tivoli Gardens); xpixel, p. 22.